GOING UP!

ELISHA OTIS'S TRIP TO THE TOP

Monica Kulling   *Illustrated by David Parkins*

TUNDRA BOOKS

For Linda and Peter,
dear friends

M.K.

Paperback edition published by Tundra Books, 2014

Text copyright © 2012 by Monica Kulling
Illustrations copyright © 2012 by David Parkins

Published in Canada by Tundra Books,
a division of Random House of Canada Limited,
One Toronto Street, Toronto, Ontario M5C 2V6

Published in the United States by Tundra Books of Northern New York,
P.O. Box 1030, Plattsburgh, New York 12901

Library of Congress Control Number: 2011938777

Library and Archives Canada Cataloguing in Publication

Kulling, Monica, 1952-, author
      Going up! : Elisha Otis's trip to the top / Monica Kulling ;
illustrated by David Parkins.

(Great idea series)
Originally published: Toronto, Ontario : Tundra Books, ©2012.
ISBN 978-1-77049-516-6 (pbk.)

      1. Otis, Elisha Graves, 1811-1861 – Juvenile literature.
2. Elevators – History – Juvenile literature. 3. Inventors – United States
– Biography – Juvenile literature. I. Parkins, David, illustrator II. Title.
III. Series: Great idea series

TJ1370.K85 2014   j621.8'77092   C2013-903541-9

We acknowledge the financial support of the Government of Canada
through the Canada Book Fund and that of the Government of Ontario
through the Ontario Media Development Corporation's Ontario Book
Initiative. We further acknowledge the support of the Canada Council
for the Arts and the Ontario Arts Council for our publishing program.

ONTARIO ARTS COUNCIL
CONSEIL DES ARTS DE L'ONTARIO

Sources of inspiration:

Goodman, Jason. *Otis: Giving Rise to the Modern City.* New York: Ivan
R. Dee, 2001.

Internet: www.invent.org (see under "Hall of Fame")

Internet: www.ideafinder.com/history/inventions/elevator.htm

Edited by Sue Tate
Designed by Leah Springate
The artwork in this book was rendered in pen and ink with watercolor
on paper.

www.tundrabooks.com

Printed and bound in China

1 2 3 4 5 6   19 18 17 16 15 14

Elevator Etiquette

Don't jab the button
again and again.
You wait for an elevator
like you wait for a train.

Turn your headphones down.
Don't whistle or hum.
There are more weird rules
where these came from.

This is the quiet room
that climbs to the top.
You choose the floor,
and that's where I'll stop.

It was haying time on the farm in Vermont. Wagons brought the bales in from the field. Then ropes and pulleys lifted them up, into the loft of the barn.

"Going up!" shouted Elisha, waving from below.

It was 1818, and Elisha Otis was seven. He loved watching farm machines at work.

The hay hoist was the most fun of all. The ropes broke often, and when they did – *SNAP!* – the hay came tumbling down.

Elisha left the farm when he was nineteen. His health was poor, so he found an easier job as a wagon driver in Troy, New York.

Elisha hauled goods between Troy and Brattleboro, Vermont, for five years. He saved every penny he could, even though he now had a wife and son to support.

One day, Elisha said to his wife, Susan, "I need a change. I'm going into business for myself."

The Otis family moved to Green River, New York, where Elisha bought some land. There he built a gristmill – a building with an enormous stone in it. The stone ground grain, or grist, into flour.

But the business went bust, and Elisha's wife became ill. When Susan died, Elisha was left with two sons, Charles and Norton. He decided to try his luck in Albany, New York, but before moving, he married again. Betsy became a good mother to the boys.

By 1845, Elisha was working in a bed-frame factory, where they made wooden bed rails by hand.

One evening at home, Elisha sat tapping a pencil on his notebook. "A machine could make a bed rail more quickly," he mumbled.

All of a sudden, Elisha had an idea! He began to draw.

Elisha showed his boss his idea.

"I call it a rail turner," he said. "It can make a rail as quick as a tick!"
Elisha's machine made bed rails four times faster than by hand.

The boss was thrilled. "Bonus time!" he exclaimed.

Elisha took the five hundred dollars, and guess what? He moved
again. This time to a city called Yonkers, on the majestic Hudson River.

In Yonkers, Elisha got work overseeing the construction of a new bed-frame factory in 1852. Heavy machinery from the ground floor had to be moved to the second floor.

Elisha didn't trust the hoisting platform. If the cable broke, it wouldn't be hay tumbling down – it would be machinery parts. People might get hurt.

Elisha thought a safety brake could work. But how? He made drawing after drawing. Then he built a working model.

Elisha attached the safety brake to the hoisting platform in the factory. Workers loaded the platform with heavy iron and lead machinery parts. The brake would catch when the cable went slack and stop the platform from hitting the ground.

"Going up!" shouted Elisha. When the platform was at the top, he yelled, "Let it fall!"

The workers looked at one another. Surely that platform was going to come crashing down!

The platform started to fall. Suddenly it stopped in midair. The brake worked! Everyone was astounded.

Elisha had finally found work he loved. He would make safety brakes for hoisting platforms.

He also decided he liked where he was living – Yonkers. No more moving for the Otis family!

One night in 1853, Elisha sat bolt upright in bed. His nightcap was askew. "We'll lift people!" he shouted.

"Lift people? Where?" mumbled a sleepy Betsy.

"We lift machine parts, why not people?" said Elisha.

"Lift people where?" Betsy repeated.

"Why, to the sky, of course! To the sky!"

At breakfast the next morning, Elisha was still excited.

"I'm going to build people-hoisting machines," he announced. "My elevators will be safe."

"Wonderful!" exclaimed Betsy.

Charles and Norton, who were now teenagers, agreed.

So Elisha built people-hoisting elevators with his safety brake attached. But his business didn't get off the ground.

People were simply not interested in being hoisted to the sky. They were afraid of falling like a ton of bricks. And who could blame them?

"Forget about going up three floors on one of those elevators," they said. "We won't go up any!"

Eventually, Elisha sold one or two of his elevators, but they were used for lifting freight, not people. No one trusted Elisha's invention.

One day, Charles and Norton came home with exciting news: "The fair is coming to town!"

Thinking about the New York World's Fair lifted the whole family's spirits. Elisha would show his elevator to the world.

In the glass-built Crystal Palace, Elisha stood on his
elevator's platform. He wasn't alone. The platform was
weighed down with wooden barrels, boxes of nuts and
bolts, and iron machine parts.

A crowd gathered below the wooden structure.
People craned their necks to see Elisha, high above them.

The crowd grew hushed. An assistant raised a gleaming saber and cut the cable. The elevator fell a few inches. The crowd gasped. *Elisha must be out of his mind*, they thought.

The elevator came to a dead stop. Elisha was perfectly safe.

The crowd was amazed. Loud cheering filled the Crystal Palace.

After the World's Fair, the Otis elevator business took off. People liked going up, the higher the better. *Hold that elevator!*

Sky High!

In 1857, Elisha Otis installed his first successful passenger elevator in the E.V. Haughwout Building, a five-storey department store at the corner of Broome Street and Broadway, in New York City. Otis's original elevator still works today, taking people up and down.

Elisha Otis died in 1861. His oldest son, Charles, was also an inventor who worked on elevator improvements. He and his brother, Norton, took over the business when their father died. They changed the name to Otis Brothers & Co.

Before Elisha's safety brake, buildings were never higher than six stories. No one wanted to live or work on the higher floors because you had to walk up all those stairs. Elisha's invention made it possible to build skyscrapers. Today, the higher the floor, the better the view. The price is higher too!